MUIR WOODS

The Ancient Redwood Forest
Near San Francisco

BY JAMES M. MORLEY

All born of stars:
these soaring trees
against the sky,
the deer and ferns
and you and I;
sharing Earth
and moon and sun,
we live the mystery
as one.

Revised edition
PUBLISHED BY SMITH-MORLEY
460 Ninth Street, San Francisco, California 94103

Library of Congress Catalog Card Number 91-62210
ISBN Number 0-938765-53-1
Printed in China

FROM THE BEGINNING

IN A SECLUDED canyon fifteen miles north of San Francisco grows the ancient forest known the world over as Muir Woods. Rising in great columns amidst ferns, flowers and companion trees below, coast redwoods (Sequoia sempervirens), remnants of a remote past, lift their shaggy crowns to the sky.

Trees with cones and foliage similar to those of the present coast redwood grew in scattered places across the Northern Hemisphere 20 to 30 million years ago. Down through the ages they survived Nature's upheavals, barely escaping annihilation during the last ice age 20,000 years ago.

Now coast redwood is found only in a narrow belt 475 miles (764 kilometers) long, reaching from the southwestern corner of Oregon to California's Big Sur country. Almost always the trees are near the ocean with its cooling fog.

One of the places conducive to survival was this valley, sheltered from prevailing westerly winds and receiving ample rainfall. Summer fog condenses on ridgetop trees and drips to the ground. Century after century the

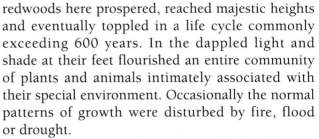

Wood rose

redwoods here prospered, reached majestic heights and eventually toppled in a life cycle commonly exceeding 600 years. In the dappled light and shade at their feet flourished an entire community of plants and animals intimately associated with their special environment. Occasionally the normal patterns of growth were disturbed by fire, flood or drought.

Onto this primeval scene, probably following others lost in the shadows of time, came the people we know as Coast Miwok. At least 2000 years ago they established villages on the nearby shores of San Francisco Bay and at other sites where their requirements of fresh water, shellfish, acorns and other foods could be found. They hunted elk, deer, antelope and small game, and they knew this canyon of redwoods.

Their first contact with Europeans came in 1579 when the English captain Francis Drake spent several weeks in their territory repairing his ship. The arrival some 200 years later of Spanish colonizers, followed by all manner of traders and adventurers, brought disas-

3

First structure in woods, built about 1885 by a fur trapper, also was used by hunters. It was torn down in 1928.

ter to the Coast Miwok. Struck down by introduced disease, removed from their land and traditional social groups, they were in steep decline by the 1830's.

In 1838 Mexico, which then administered this region, issued to an American settler a grant of land called Rancho Saucelito (Little Willow Ranch), which included Muir Woods. What had been wildlands became subject to such private uses as grazing and tree cutting.

Logging of redwoods for construction in San Francisco (then Yerba Buena) began about this time in places that were handy to water transportation. Fortunately Muir Woods was isolated. A gentle valley led west to the ocean, but the cove there (now Muir Beach) was a rough landing place. On the east, a high ridge blocked the way to San Francisco Bay. And so the virgin forest was spared. A few small trees were cut in the 1860's, probably by settlers who split them up for fence posts.

By the late 1880's horseback riders began to make the trek from the nearby town of Mill Valley to see what was then known as Redwood or Sequoia Canyon. Word of the great trees spread.

In 1903 a move to make most of adjacent Mount Tamalpais a national park flared and died. By then more efficient logging and transportation methods had made the cutting of the woods feasible. The owners of the canyon felt they no longer could afford to simply hold such valuable timber. So they approached William Kent, a local man well known for his desire to save the natural features of the area, and asked him to buy the woods in order to save them.

Kent's wife demurred at the idea of the purchase, but he replied that if they lost all the money they had and saved the trees it would be worthwhile. He found the required $45,000 and in 1905 the forest was his. Had he failed, the San Francisco earthquake and fire of 1906, with the consequent demand for lumber to rebuild, surely would have doomed the redwoods.

The scenic railway that ran to the top of Mount Tamalpais built a branch line down to the edge of Muir Woods in 1907. Later that year, just when things appeared to be going well, a new threat arose. Under a law giving priority to domestic water supplies, a local water company brought suit to condemn most of the canyon for a reservoir.

Kent already had been wondering how to safeguard the woods permanently. Providentially, Congress in 1906 had passed the Act for the Preservation of American Antiquities. This allowed the President to set aside, and to accept as gifts from individuals, lands containing "objects of historic or scientific interest".

Learning of this, Kent began a campaign (through Gifford Pinchot, then U.S. Chief Forester) to convince President Theodore Roosevelt that Redwood Canyon should be set aside. This would put it out of reach of the water company. No doubt it helped that Roosevelt was conservation-minded. Kent was successful and on January 9, 1908 the President proclaimed his gift a National Monument.

Roosevelt wanted to name it the Kent Monument, but Kent wished to honor the renowned conservationist John Muir and won out. Muir was delighted and wrote Kent his profuse appreciation for "saving these woods from the axe and the saw".

Had Kent failed, the redwoods surely would have been doomed.

Log dam to slow erosion was built in 1930's.

MUIR WOODS

Muir Woods lies eight airline miles (13 kilometers) northwest of the Golden Gate. The Monument's 554 acres (224 hectares) of forest are nestled in a canyon on the southern flank of Mount Tamalpais, pronounced *Tam'l-pye-iss.* This may be a Spanish name referring to local Indians, or an Indian name meaning mountain of the west (or coast) people. Elevation of East Peak, at the far right, is 2571 feet (784 meters) above sea level; elevation of the canyon bottom is about 160 feet (49 meters).

The mountain was created by the uplifting of a complex mix of rocks in mysterious ways. Ridgetops on the left and right sides of Redwood Canyon were part of a low, rolling plain perhaps one million years ago. As crustal forces gradually lifted this surface, water and wind eroded the softer rocks to form this canyon. Nobody knows when redwoods began to colonize it.

Although redwoods predominate, many of the trees on upper slopes are Douglas firs. Grassland yellows as the dry summer begins.

5

John Muir's Letter of Thanks to William Kent

Martinez, Feb. 6, 1908

Dear Mr. Kent,

Seeing my name in the tender and deed of the Tamalpais Sequoias was a surprise of the pleasantest kind. This is the best tree-lover's monument that could possibly be found in all the forests of the world. You have done me great honor, and I am proud of it. Schools here and there have planted "Muir trees" in their playgrounds, and long ago Asa Gray named several plants for me, the most interesting of which is a sturdy frost-enduring daisy that I discovered on the shore of the Arctic Ocean near Icy Cape; a Sierra peak also and one of the Alaska glaciers bears my name, but these aboriginal woods, barring human action, will outlast them all, even the mountain and glacier. Compared with Sequoia glaciers are young fleeting things, and since the first Sequoia forests lifted their domes and spires to the sky, mountains great and small, thousands of them, have been weathered, ground down, washed away and cast into the sea, while two of the many species of Sequoia have come safely through all the geological change and storms that have fallen upon them since Cretaceous times, surviving even the crushing, destroying ice sheets of the glacial period.

Saving these woods from the axe and saw, from money-changers and water-changers, and giving them to our country and the world is in many ways the most notable service to God and man I've heard of since my forest wandering began, a much needed lesson and blessing to saint and sinner alike, and a credit and encouragement to God. That so fine divine a thing should have come out of money-mad Chicago! Wha wad 'a' thocht it! Immortal Sequoia life to you.

Ever Yours, John Muir

Gravity car carrying visitors coasts down scenic railway to edge of Muir Woods in early days.

Early visitors pose on fallen redwood.

Great blue heron fishes Redwood Creek.

The new Monument got off to a slow start. No official funds were available and Kent paid the custodian's salary for the first two years. It was no easy task for one man to enforce the regulations, which among other things barred fires, firearms, fishing, damaging of vegetation, disorderly conduct and saloons.

Early visitors came on foot, on horseback, in buggies; but mostly they came by railroad. Its terminus was on the side of the canyon a mile upstream from the present entrance. Rail operations ceased in 1929 and heaviest visitor use then shifted to the area near the parking lots.

Automobiles first reached the woods over a wagon road from Mill Valley, perhaps as early as 1908. In 1925 a toll road was built on the present grade winding down from the ridge to the Monument. This road became public in 1939, opening the way for a rush of cars. Access to the area had been greatly improved in 1937 with the opening of the Golden Gate Bridge, which replaced ferry boats from San Francisco.

At first use of the woods was casual despite regulations. Vehicles passed the length of the canyon and people wandered everywhere. This destroyed ground cover plants and compacted the soil so severely that in places vegetation has not returned to this day. Cattle from a nearby ranch sometimes drifted into the woods.

In 1924 automobiles were excluded from the woods proper, the start of a gradually increasing effort to protect the fragile understory growth. Today main trails are fenced and ground cover is

Early use of the woods was hard on the forest floor.

7

making an impressive recovery. Emphasis is now on the entire ecosystem and not just the tall trees.

Many changes have occurred in the region's web of life since Coast Miwok times. Gone are the elk, antelope, coyotes, grizzly bears and most mountain lions. Skies are empty of condors. Spawning runs in Redwood Creek have dwindled drastically. Bay marshes are mostly filled now. Wildfires are suppressed, thus modifying natural processes.

Non-native plants such as broom (a shrub) and forget-me-not (a ground cover) have invaded the area. These crowd out native shrubs and ground covers unless removed; keeping the Monument an island of natives in an ocean of alien seed will be difficult. Bay Area smog may have long-term effects. And how the forest will fare in global warming is unknown.

But for now the redwoods and their companions thrive, and Muir Woods occupies a special position in the national park system. A patch of near-wilderness close to an international crossroads, it fronts on the world. Travelers make a point of visiting here, and many languages are heard on the trails. It is a showcase for the concept of national parks, a splendid example of the virtues of preserving the grand things of Nature.

In early morning a poet stands on a bridge and recites his latest odes; in the last light of day a small group strolls through deepening shadows, lost in philosophical discussion. In between are the hikers, the sightseers, the naturalists, the lovers, the families exercising children. Muir Woods, fragment of an ancient forest, gift of a thoughtful man and his wife, is theirs to enjoy.

California hazels, early winter

William Kent

Political reformer, conservationist, and sponsor of legislation that created the National Park Service, he left the world a better place than he found it. Born in Chicago in 1864, he spent many boyhood years at the family's second home near the northern base of Mount Tamalpais, at the place now called Kentfield. At Yale he met Elizabeth Thacher, whom he married in 1890; they had five sons and two daughters.

Independently wealthy, he jumped into Chicago politics as an alderman, and his exploits fighting municipal corruption were recorded by muckraker Lincoln Steffens. In 1907 the family settled permanently in Kentfield, and Kent assisted in the prosecution of San Francisco's notorious grafter Abe Ruef. Active in the Progressive Party, he helped elect Hiram Johnson governor and was himself elected congressman in 1910.

To provide better administration for the growing number of national parks and monuments, friends of the parks prepared legislation to establish a National Park Service. Kent introduced the bill, which was passed and signed in 1916. The next year he left Congress to press for freer international trade; helped found the Save-the-Redwoods League in 1918; gave more land to Muir Woods; ran for the Senate but was defeated.

As an influential citizen he continued to work for his ideas, one of which was a state park adjoining Muir Woods. The California Legislature in 1927 created both a State Park system and Mount Tamalpais State Park. Kent donated the land containing jewel-like Steep Ravine (one mile west of Muir Woods), and died in 1928.

John Muir

His perceptive descriptions of nature awakened people to the need to save something of America's wilderness for future generations. Born in 1838 at Dunbar, Scotland, he was eleven when the family moved to Wisconsin to homestead a farm. Despite heavy work and harsh treatment, he read a great deal and invented wooden clocks and other instruments. Leaving home to exhibit these at a state fair, he moved on to study geology and botany at the University of Wisconsin.

After short rambles, factory jobs, and an eye injury that diverted him from machinery to nature, in 1867 Muir walked a thousand miles from Indiana to the Gulf of Mexico, botanizing. Further travels brought him to Yosemite Valley, his headquarters while he studied plants and glacial activity of the Sierra Nevada and explored the West. Following a trip to Alaska he married Louie Strentzel in 1880. The Muirs had two daughters and lived on the Strentzel ranch near Martinez. (Their home is now a National Historic Site.)

Out of more treks and his enthusiasm for conservation came a wealth of eloquent writing and personal persuasion that were instrumental in establishing Yosemite National Park, other parks and monuments, and the United States Forest Service. In 1892 the Sierra Club was founded with Muir as its first president.

In a final struggle, the rugged Scot fought to keep Hetch Hetchy Valley, in Yosemite National Park, from being made a reservoir. (Ironically, William Kent was in the enemy camp.) The battle was lost in 1913, and the next year, exhausted, John Muir died of pneumonia.

New cones embellish redwood crown.

THE COAST REDWOOD

POSSESSING a regenerative life force proba- bly greater than that of any other tree, the coast redwood (*Sequoia sempervirens*, ever- green sequoia) is indeed a wonder of the plant kingdom. Its longevity, size, method of reproduc- tion and resistance to decay are remarkable. It is the tallest species of tree on Earth.

The tallest redwood in Muir Woods is 254 feet (77 meters) high and its top is lost among its fel- lows in Bohemian Grove. Average height of red- woods on the canyon floor, where size is greatest, is about 220 feet (67 meters). A day's drive to the north, several coast redwoods vie for the title of world's tallest tree at about 370 feet (113 meters). There may have been taller trees of this and other species in the many ancient forests of the world already gone.

For all its height, coast redwood is neither the oldest nor the largest tree on the globe. Average age at maturity is 500 to 600 years. Its maximum known

Burl sprout

growth of 2200 years is equaled by a Huon pine in Tasmania, and is easily surpassed by the giant sequoia (*Sequoiadendron giganteum*). Also called big tree or Sierra redwood, this marvel grows in the mountains 180 miles (290 kilometers) east of Muir Woods, and is the world's bulkiest tree. It can live at least 3200 years, and John Muir found one he thought was 4000 years old. The little-known alerces tree of Chile has reached 3600 years. All yield to the 4900 years attained by a bristlecone pine (a small, rugged tree) in Nevada.

Sequoia lineage is not as ancient as once thought. Fossils of plants with some sequoia-like features go back almost 120 million years, but their connection with the two modern sequoias is uncertain. Probably coast redwood and giant sequoia had a com- mon ancestor that is now extinct, but fossil proof has not yet been found.

Both trees bear cones, leading many to believe they are members of the pine

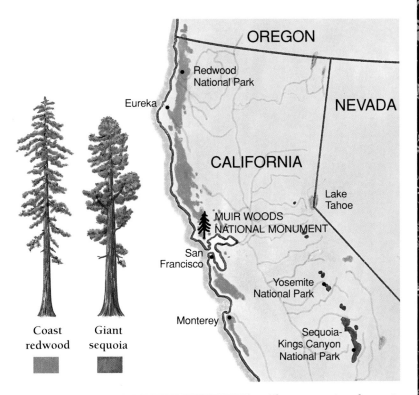

Coast
redwood

Giant
sequoia

The two species of sequoia grow in quite different habitats: coast redwood in the mild coastal climate, giant sequoia in the harsher elevations of inland mountains. At left, men cut a roadway through this giant sequoia near Yosemite in 1881 and it became famous as the Wawona Tunnel Tree. It fell in 1969. At right, coast redwood displays hallmark height. Below is a coast redwood fossilized by volcanic action some three million years ago near Santa Rosa, 50 miles (80 kilometers) north of Muir Woods.

Not all redwoods are alike. Genetic variations produce different foliage colors, branch structures and bark textures. At bottom is the rare curly bark, known to occur at only three places in the Monument. This example is on the loop path near the Pinchot Tree.

family. In fact they belong to the taxodium family (*Taxodiaceae*), which includes 15 or possibly 16 species around the world. One of these is China's dawn redwood, once thought to be extinct, and another is the bald cypress of the southeastern United States.

Coast redwood, in a manner rare among strictly cone-bearing trees, reproduces both from seed and by sprouting from normally dormant buds at the base of the trunk or stem. The tree's crown produces a hormone called auxin that suppresses bud sprouting. Damage to the tree stops the hormone flow and sprouting then can occur. Stumps also can sprout. Even the trunk of a fallen tree may send up shoots, although these cannot grow into trees unless they have access to the root system.

The trees produce a tremendous amount of seed, most of which is not capable of germinating. Each tree is bisexual, bearing both male and female reproductive organs. Pollination occurs in January and February. The cones mature until they open the following autumn or early winter. Seeds drift down by the thousands, but seldom sprout on the forest floor with its covering of decaying leaves; they do better on open soil. The few that do sprout may not survive the next summer's dryness.

Coast redwoods grow as fully developed forests in the wet northern country and as a few trees tucked into tiny canyons at the drier southern end of their range. They can be cultivated in

"…because none of the expedition recognizes them they are named redwood…"

mild climates and are grown ornamentally in Europe and New Zealand, and commercially in southern France.

Local Coast Miwoks gave the tree a name roughly pronounced *cho*-lay. European naming of the tree began in 1769, when Don Gaspar de Portolá led a Spanish land expedition north from San Diego and stumbled onto San Francisco Bay. Near the present town of Watsonville they noted "... very high trees of a red color . . .because none of the expedition recognizes them they are named redwood (*palo colorado*) . . ."

The first botanist to encounter the redwood was Thaddeus Haenke, an Austrian accompanying the Spanish scientific expedition led by Alejandro Malaspina in 1791. Haenke briefly described the tree but apparently did not scientifically classify it.

Finally, following an English attempt to classify it, in 1847 the Hungarian botanist Stephan Endlicher established the genus *Sequoia*. This generic name honors the Cherokee Indian Sequoyah, famous for inventing a written language of syllables for his people.

Contributing to the long life of coast redwood is its great resistance to insects, rot and fire. The

Six-foot (two-meter) diameter cross-section shows annual rings for 1,021 years from 909 A.D. to 1930, when the tree, small for its age, was cut down farther north. Painted rings indicate historical events: inner ring, 1100, building of cliff dwellings begins at Mesa Verde, Colorado; 1325, Aztecs begin construction of Tenochitlan, Mexico; 1492, Columbus lands in America; 1776, U.S. Declaration of Independence is signed.

Below, redwood roots exposed by flood. There is no taproot; the tangle of roots directly under the tree normally goes down only six or eight feet, but roots can seek water at greater depths. Lateral roots radiate from the base 50 feet (15 meters) or more. Normally dormant buds around the base of the tree sprout when tree is injured.

Left, a spray of sun foliage on heartwood of storm-felled redwood (note white sapwood). Such foliage grows on upper part of mature redwoods. The small, tight leaves, or needles, reduce evaporation of moisture.

Below, actual size, are tree's reproductive organs called strobili, at time of pollination. Wind-blown pollen from speckled male strobili along branchlets is deposited within female strobili (conelets) at branchlet tips. At bottom is pollen sample.

At left, normal green sprouts at base of tree. Right, rare albino redwood, a genetic mutation found at three places in Monument. Pure white sprouts have no chlorophyll, thus cannot manufacture food and eventually die.

Suddenly most of the ancient redwood forests are gone.

presence of tannic acid may help repel insects and fungi; the absence of resin makes the wood relatively difficult to ignite. These qualities have made it valuable commercially in spite of its softness and brittleness. Redwood has been used for such things as house decks, shingles, siding, posts, pipelines and wine-vats. Robert Louis Stevenson used it to line the main room of his home in far-off Samoa in 1891.

Demand for its lumber has overwhelmed admiration for the living tree. Over 90% of the great coast redwood forests known to the Native Americans have been felled, replaced by second growth or a new use of the land. When the United States westward migration began to arrive about 1848 there were some two million acres (809,389 hectares) of redwood-dominated forests. Of these ancient forests about 80,000 acres (32,375 hectares), or 4% of the original area, are now protected in hard-won parks and preserves. (Other protected redwood habitat involves logged areas.) As the few remaining commercial ancient forests are cut down, these parklands will contain all that is left of a unique primeval gift with secrets we may never know.

14

Cones mature to size shown at right in about nine months. In ways not fully understood, cells of growing tissue can be instructed to become a cone, stem or leaf. In rare cases the cells receive new instructions and resume stem growth beyond the cone, as in the one example. Cones dry out to release about 30 to 100 flake-like seeds which are so light that up to 200,000 are needed to make a pound (.45 kilogram).

A WALK IN THE WOODS

LEAVING automotive commotion behind, the visitor enters a quiet world of winding paths, shady corridors and glistening pools. There is the fun of comparing the redwoods with trees of everyday experience; the old-fashioned pleasure of taking an easy walk in a beautiful place; the chance to become more aware of surroundings, of light on leaves, water on stone. And always there is a sense of continuity, a feeling of time past and time future and of humanity's place in the scheme of things.

The Monument is open from 8 A.M. to sunset; the first hour offers the best chance for solitude. The canyon almost always is cool, so warm clothing is desirable. Comfortable walking shoes are useful, although main trails are hard-surfaced. An hour provides a good look at the woods, but many hours can be spent exploring the area. Hikes up Mount Tamalpais can start here.

Rainy weather offers the chance to rove uncrowded trails in a land of misty fantasy and shining ferns. Only at the height of exceptionally violent storms are the woods ever closed during the day.

Sunbeams are best in early autumn haze and the day after a rain in early winter, when ground vapor often condenses in the air and intercepts the rays. Deer are most likely to be seen from May to October. Each season has its delights, and every visit offers at least subtle changes from the previous one. The drama of Earth's voyage around the sun can be seen in countless small ways in this mild climate. Here in winter the last leaves fall even as the first flower is about to bloom.

As you walk, you might wish to consider the trees as individuals. After riding a tree top in a gale, John Muir reflected that trees, although rooted to one spot, make many small journeys during their lives, not entirely unlike ourselves. And each has had its larger experience: good or poor exposure to light, touched or spared by fire, roots intact or undercut by flood. Perhaps they will speak to you in some way.

On the following pages are the main elements of interest, then the changing aspects of the woods through the year, and finally a look at trees of the lower canyon.

Fairybells

17

Bay Laurel

Sharpening the fragrance of the forest is the spiciness of bay. This tree is botanically a laurel, but its several popular names include pepperwood and Oregon myrtle. The dense wood is worked into novelties often sold as myrtlewood.

Related to the Grecian laurel whose leaves found their way into both cooking pots and crowns of honor, the California variety has much the same aromatic qualities. The Coast Miwok used the leaves medicinally and harvested the thin-shelled fruit (left, actual size) for its single large seed which they roasted and ate. Locally they called the tree *sow*-las.

Here in the canyon the bay laurel is engaged in a desperate struggle for sunlight, sending up slender trunks that bend or fall under top-heavy foliage. If the roots still provide sustenance, new branches arise vertically in a renewed quest for light.

18

Wherever coast redwoods stand on alluvial flats such as this one along Redwood Creek, the ground normally is covered by Oregon oxalis, commonly called redwood sorrel. More romantically it is one of several three-leaved plants grouped under the non-botanical name of shamrock. Despite its appearance, it is not a clover. Leaves fold down when stressed by direct sun and certain storm conditions.

In the early decades of the Monument unrestricted human traffic destroyed ground cover plants. Limiting visitors to a few paths has allowed redwood sorrel to again carpet much of the forest floor.

Redwood Sorrel

Family Circle

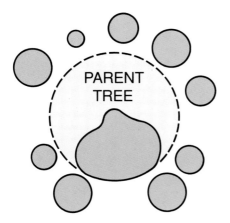

PARENT TREE

Surrounded by its thriving offspring, the fire-scarred stump of this parent redwood continues to stand 200 years after its death. When alive it stood alone. When it perished, probably by fire, a ring of protected underground bud tissue around the base of the tree sent up sprouts and a new generation thrust skyward. (This reservoir of life is sometimes called a bud collar or basal burl.)

Family circles can be found throughout Muir Woods, although they seldom are as obvious as this one. In many cases the parent tree has disappeared entirely, burned away by successive fires.

Fire Scars

Repeated fires, large and small, have left their marks nearly everywhere in Muir Woods. Often a charred surface looks as fresh as yesterday, but new growth around the edges shows it happened long ago. On the canyon floor the last big blaze occurred in the early 1800's; on the slopes it came in the mid-1800's.

Before European settlement, fires presumably were started by lightning higher on Mount Tamalpais or by Indians on adjacent grassland, and then burned into the forest. Fire frequency then is thought to have been four or five a century, at least ten times higher than in wetter forests to the north. In historic times several fires on the mountain have scorched the edges of the Monument.

Outer fibers of dry redwood bark ignite readily but thick, dense bark of mature trees insulates the thin layer of growing tissue called the cambium. Nevertheless a hot fire in forest debris can ravage the bark and heat and kill the cambium and sapwood beneath. Successive fires may eat through to the heartwood and in time hollow out the tree.

Fire's complex role includes opening new areas to the sun, converting ground litter into fertilizing ash, and killing insect infestations. Some parks are making efforts to replicate this natural process by burning small areas under controlled conditions. In such prescribed burns, at top (right), flames consume undergrowth in upper forest of Muir Woods; (left), heartwood glows in a park farther north.

21

Swordfern

The arching pattern of common swordfern is found throughout the canyon, sometimes in single clumps and sometimes in masses covering entire banks. The name comes from the hilt-like projection near the base of each leaflet, giving it the appearance of a tiny sword.

Undersides may be covered with rows of fruit-dots containing spore cases. Ferns reproduce through an intermediate stage; the released spores will produce tiny plants that in turn will produce new ferns.

This ubiquitous understory tree, also called tanbark oak, varies in size from small bush to this big-limbed specimen. In earlier times its bark, rich in tannic acid, was widely gathered to brew a solution used to convert raw hides into leather. Large trees were cut down and small trees were stripped as high as a man could reach, thus killing them. (Tanoaks within the Monument evidently escaped this fate.)

Native people considered tanoak acorns to be especially flavorful. They removed the outer husk, ground the kernels (right), leached the flour to remove bitterness, and cooked it into a mush. Local Miwoks called the tree kah-*tah*-may.

Deer relish the acorns and avidly nose them out of the forest litter in late fall.

Acorns of all kinds were a favorite food of the California grizzly bear.

Tanoak

A Gift of Centuries

Although much less massive than their giant sequoia cousins, coast redwoods nevertheless can attain respectable size. The largest one in Muir Woods is 13½ feet (4 meters) in diameter at chest height. As seen from the path, two trees appear to rise from a single base. These are two entirely separate trees and the measurement applies to the right-hand one. Height of its fine column is about 220 feet or 67 meters (not the tallest redwood in the Monument), and its weight is an estimated 275 tons or 250 tonnes.

Diameter is not a reliable indicator of age. But quite possibly this giant began life as a tender shoot about 1500 years ago, while Goths and Vandals pillaged the crumbling Roman Empire.

Hillside View

Opposite page: Early morning sun strikes redwoods rising from the base of the steep west hillside. The path crosses a clearing in the forest to allow this view, the most open one along the trails.

The Residents

Several forest creatures make occasional appearances. In summer blacktail does and fawns descend to the canyon floor to browse; in fall a mate-seeking buck might even walk a redwood log (below). Sonoma chipmunks busily forage (opposite). Western gray squirrels (left) whisk about, and sometimes strip redwood bark for their nests.

Humped tunnels of moles can be found along trail edges. The banana slug (opposite) is common. Raccoons, foxes, bobcats, wood rats and skunks are nocturnal and thus seldom seen. Mountain lions apparently exist but are extremely secretive. Bears were killed off by the 1880's.

Birds are more plentiful than generally believed, although both insects and food seeds are somewhat scarce in a redwood forest. Some species stay year-round while others are seasonal visitors. Common are the winter wren (opposite, top), Steller's jay (left), brown creeper, brown towhee, hermit thrush and robin. High above the forest huge ravens send forth their raucous cries. Once in a while a great blue heron wanders in from salt water margins. A rare bird indeed is the northern spotted owl (opposite, one-third life size), true symbol of an ancient forest.

Numbers of each species vary as food supplies, disease and other factors work their ways.

". . . they are other nations, caught with ourselves in the net of life and time, fellow prisoners of the splendour and travail of the earth."
—*Naturalist Henry Beston*

Winter wren stays year-round. The ending of its complex spring territorial song is shown in sonogram form indicating rapidity and intensity of notes. Below, a chipmunk stuffs cow parsnip seeds into its cheek pouches, and a banana slug enjoys a moist day. Right, spotted owl awaits dusk, when it will fly silently off in search of its favorite prey, the dusky-footed wood rat. This is southern limit of owl's range, which extends north into Canada.

Bohemian Grove

Here in 1892, 16 years before the woods became a National Monument, artist and writer members of the Bohemian Club of San Francisco gathered for their festive one-night summer encampment. For the occasion they built (at right) a 43-foot (13-meter) high replica of the renowned *Daibutsu,* or great Buddha, of Kamakura, Japan; nothing now remains.

The group had considered buying the property but the raw evening cold defeated the plan. Later the club acquired for its activities a redwood grove on the Russian River in warmer country to the north. That place also is known as Bohemian Grove.

Beside the path stands the time-scoured shell of the base of a redwood. On the ground on the opposite page is a 600-year old redwood that toppled on a calm day in 1984, rotted out at the base.

In this grove visitors walk among the Monument's tallest trees.

On Canyon Slopes

Redwoods on the sides of the canyon often are scattered amidst thickets of tanoak (opposite page). Douglas firs frequently add to the mix.

Three trails give access to these slopes. Most popular is the Hillside Trail (top), an easy walk. The Ben Johnson Trail (left) climbs steeply past huckleberry bushes to the western ridgetop. Ascending the drier opposite slope, the Panoramic Trail passes through a redwood "pole forest" (above). Such groves apparently were caused by fire from bordering brush or grassland periodically killing the young, thin-barked trees. New trees then grew either from live underground tissue or from wind-blown seed.

The Crossing

Once there were 14 footbridges spanning Redwood Creek within the woods. Time, floods and restriction of people to main trails reduced the number to four. This crossing at Bohemian Grove is the apex of the loop followed by most visitors. The stone embankment on the right was built in the 1930's, when the Civilian Conservation Corps lined much of the creek with rock (quarried outside the woods) to control erosion. Policies are different now; as the stonework breaks down it will not be repaired and the stream will be allowed to determine its own course.

At right, John Muir on an early bridge.

Some redwoods have a curiously swollen base, as in the extreme example shown above, or have a knob on the trunk as at right. Little is known about the causes; much is in dispute. A burl at the base may be normal for that particular tree, or it may be an abnormal enlargement of the usual base tissue containing buds that sprout when the tree is injured. Trunk burls have no apparent rationale.

Both types contain much bud growth. These buds are the growing tips of tissue usually put to other purposes; why they go astray remains a mystery. Genetics or a hormonal imbalance may be at work, and the process can begin at any stage of a tree's life. Apparently burls cause no harm except to divert resources from other growth. Coast redwood seems to be the only conifer to commonly form burls, but many hardwoods have this trait.

Large burls from logged redwoods are made into novelties that display the bud patterns (below). Small burls and sections of burls are sold as sprouting buds. When placed in water, these put forth fern-like sprouts and may remain alive three or four years. If planted, only rarely will one strike root and grow into a tree.

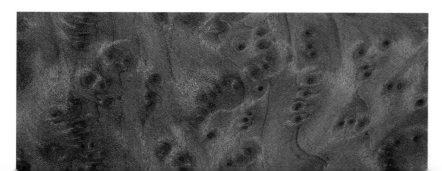

Burls

33

Cathedral Grove

"The great shafts rise in natural majesty from a handsomely varied undergrowth, and here and there stand individual groups, like the side chapels of a cathedral, with high rose-windows opening to the sky, rich with tracery of twig, and branch, and plumy spray." Thus an early writer touched on the European familiar.

At right is a redwood top that broke off, crashed down and buried one end deep in the earth. A park volunteer is reading the nearby plaque that recalls a historic gathering. As World War II neared its end, delegates from all over the world came to San Francisco to form the United Nations. One day they met here (below).

HERE IN THIS GROVE OF ENDURING REDWOODS, PRESERVED FOR POSTERITY, MEMBERS OF THE UNITED NATIONS CONFERENCE ON INTERNATIONAL ORGANIZATION MET ON MAY 19, 1945 TO HONOR THE MEMORY OF FRANKLIN DELANO ROOSEVELT, THIRTY-FIRST PRESIDENT OF THE UNITED STATES, CHIEF ARCHITECT OF THE UNITED NATIONS AND APOSTLE OF PEACE FOR ALL MANKIND.

Overleaf: Morning, Cathedral Grove

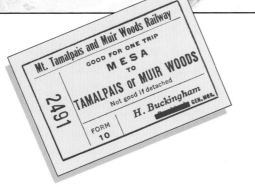

Mt. Tamalpais and Muir Woods Railway

GOOD FOR ONE TRIP

MESA

TO

TAMALPAIS or MUIR WOODS

Not good if detached

2491

H. Buckingham GEN. MGR.

FORM 10

Where the World Rushed In

Construction of a railroad to the edge of Muir Woods in 1907, capped by a lodge in 1908, brought in the world. From the hillside terminus of Muir Inn thousands of sightseers once walked or rode down the now-abandoned road shown below, eager to behold the wonders of Redwood Canyon. The grade meets the canyon floor near Fern Creek and the heavy use of that area is reflected in the present scarcity of ground cover.

The first inn (above) burned in 1913. Then the tracks were extended farther down to a new inn, also gone now. Increased automobile use and a destructive fire higher on the mountain in 1929 put the railroad out of business. The site of the first inn, on state park land, is now occupied by Camp Alice Eastwood, a picnic spot named for a famous local botanist who knew the mountain well.

Leading up a side canyon to the Kent Tree and thence to Camp Alice Eastwood, this trail passes through a glade beneath a large bigleaf maple, a tree that stays close to streams.

Ferns are not as numerous as the name implies; many plants may have been taken in early years. But there are specimens of the giant chainfern (left), named for its size and for the link-shaped spore clusters on the underside.

Fern Creek Trail

Kent Tree

Afternoon sun pierces a veil of ground mist along the Fern Creek Trail to reveal the solid form of the Kent Tree. This, of all the trees in Muir Woods, was William Kent's favorite.

Surprisingly it is not a redwood but a Douglas fir, usually found on upper slopes instead of here in the canyon depths. Once it measured 273 feet (83 meters), the tallest tree in the Monument. The top broke off and now it is 224 feet (68 meters). Age is about 350 years.

Douglas fir mingles with redwood in the northern coastal counties of California, and is widely distributed elsewhere in the western United States. Here in the Monument it prefers relatively dry places, and grows as a fringe along much of the upper edge of the redwood forest.

The species has extensive commercial use varying from the familiar Christmas tree to construction beams. In Spanish times the sturdy trunks served as spare masts for Manila galleons carrying treasures of the Far East to Mexico.

In 1908 John Muir walked this trail and posed beside the tree.

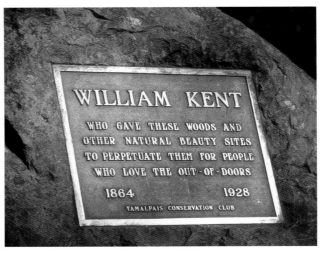

THE CIRCLING YEAR

Summer Comes

AS SUMMER SOLSTICE approaches during Earth's journey around the sun, the lengthening days bring vast atmospheric changes. New winds blowing down the coast pull ocean currents with them, and these currents create an upwelling of colder water from the depths. Moisture-laden air passes over the cooled surface and condenses into great soft blankets of fog that slide in from the sea to break in ghostly turmoil against the hills.

Under cover of darkness a mantle of mist has filled Redwood Canyon, to be revealed by sunrise light. By noon much of it will have vanished into the warming day.

". . . what glorious cloudlands I should see . . .
a new heaven and a new earth every day."
—*John Muir*

Summer now is in full stride. Leaves of a big-leaf maple crown (above) are industriously producing food for this deciduous tree's season of growth. It has the largest leaves of any American maple.

Here and there along the creek western azalea blossoms (left) perfume the air. Occasionally a blacktail fawn can be seen apart from its mother as it momentarily ventures into the world alone.

Beneath the Canopy

From a Lost World

Beside the summer creek banks grow feathery stands of a strange plant descended from very ancient times. Radiating from the brittle stem of giant horsetail, or equisetum, are dozens of tiny branches, not leaves. Both stems and branches store a large amount of silica, giving the horsetail a gritty texture much favored for scouring pots and pans in pioneer days.

Now reaching heights of up to three feet (one meter), its elemental structure conjures up visions of primal splendor 300 million years ago, when equisetum grew as a tree 50 to 100 feet (15 to 30 meters) tall. Then the land was covered by immense swamp forests, Earth's coal beds were being laid down, and the world was inhabited by primitive insects and by amphibious creatures emerging from the ooze.

At stream's edge are a ladyfern and the orange blooms of sticky monkeyflower.

In the mild riffles and quiet pools of summer, creatures of the stream feed and grow and compete for life. At top, a crayfish prowls in search of plant or animal matter. When threatened, this scavenger uses its broad tail to scull backward to safety under a rock.

Above, a fingerling heads into the current and waits, alert for food and danger. It likely hatched in March or April, and has the apparent markings of a steelhead trout. On its way to the sea next winter or the winter after, it will change for ocean life and will record the stream's unique chemistry to help it return here for spawning. But that journey may never come; one hazard is the occasional visit of a great blue heron.

At right, a water strider casts its characteristic refraction shadow.

Life in the Stream

Summer Wanes

Elk clover, or California aralia (opposite page) is one of the last plants to bloom. In early summer a panoply of large, richly green leaves arises out of the tawny ruin of last year's growth. Stalks thrust upward and in early August break into clusters of tiny white flowers which develop into berries that darken as they mature.

Nature insures wide distribution of the seeds within the pulp by enlisting the appetites of birds; the hermit thrush for one furtively plucks the berries from the heavily-laden stalks.

At top, redwoods shed a few needles in a random pattern. Each discarded branchlet contains several years' growth.

At right, ladybird beetles, better known as ladybugs, begin to arrive in Muir Woods in early summer. Usually at the end of September they gather in dense clusters, using the same sites year after year. They have a one-year life cycle and are believed to migrate to and from California's Central Valley with the wind. No one knows how they find their way back to exactly the same clustering spots in the Coast Range and Sierra Nevada.

Below, poison oak announces the changing season with a scattering of scarlet in open places. Spiders add their gossamer touches to the woods as summer draws to a close.

49

A Touch of Autumn

By late September the fog comes less frequently, a warm haze fills the canyon, and suddenly the days are shorter and nights colder. A bigleaf maple becomes a splash of gold in the forest (opposite page). Then maple and alder leaves begin to drift downstream and collect behind fragile dams of redwood needles.

As autumn deepens, blacktail bucks appear on the canyon floor to pursue does and occasionally do battle. Muzzles have whitened and older bucks take on a distinctly bull-like countenance.

50

The October-April rainy season usually begins with a few light rains quickly absorbed by the dry ground. Late autumn brings heavier weather and once in a while a truly great storm moves in from the Pacific Ocean. After a quiet prelude, with barely perceptible thickening of the atmosphere to dim the sky, the wind begins to rise and airy gusts feel out the canyon.

Fine drops, gradually becoming larger, sift through the leaves and wash away the last of summer's dust. The soft patter becomes a steady drumming intruding on the wind. A coastal woodfern (above) bears glistening beads. Tops of redwoods sway wildly, shaking loose millions of

Storm

seeds to float earthward. Bay laurels bend and whip and lash about, sending their fruits rattling down like hail.

Then the wind dies away but the downpour continues. Quickly the ground becomes soaked, and normally dry side streams come alive and rush toward Redwood Creek. With a watershed draining a third of Mount Tamalpais, the creek is quite sensitive to the onslaught. Soon its murmur grows to a roar, and silt stains the water as the age-old process of down-cutting the canyon is renewed.

Above is the Dipsea Trail crossing in the lower canyon, and at right the second bridge in the woods, during an exceptionally severe storm in 1982.

Morning light breaks into the canyon to illuminate a brief display of ever-changing splendor. Soon the chill air will begin to warm and the mist will evaporate, ending the storm's pageantry. There have been a few victims, such as this redwood and bay laurel. Bay laurels, with their top-heavy branches, are especially vulnerable. Silt has been deposited on parts of the canyon floor, burying leaf litter and changing the soil composition.

Aftermath

Home From
the Sea

Muir
Woods

4 miles
6.5 km

Lagoon

Muir
Beach

Storm waters play a vital role in the life cycle of the fish in Redwood Creek. Coho or silver salmon and steelhead or sea-run rainbow trout spawn here each winter. Each summer the sea builds a sandbar across the creek's outlet at Muir Beach. The trickling stream forms a lagoon behind the bar and sinks into the sand. Autumn rains swell the creek until it breaks through, allowing an exchange of life between stream and ocean.

A great many of the stream's surviving young fish, some hatched last spring, others (mostly steelhead) holdovers from the year before, prepare for life in salt water and go into the sea. Adult fish waiting offshore spent an average of two or three years feeding and growing in the Pacific. Ready to spawn, they found their way here by unknown means. Now they sense the unique chemistry of the stream where they were born, enter, and begin the last leg of the journey home. Nature has led them back to a spawning site that worked before, one that will not dry up in summer.

At first they may swim only part way upstream, lying without feeding until a new spate urges them on. In the 1930's a run of 200 fish was normal. Now 20 fish make a large run, which often comes after a heavy rain in late December or mid-January, and may be followed by smaller runs later in the winter. As a rule salmon make up most of the first run, with steelhead coming later.

They distribute themselves along the creek, some going well above the fourth bridge, a few moving up Fern Creek. A flash of rose or outright red gives away the male salmon, whose silver sides have changed color for this final drama. The

Top, female turns on side and flaps tail to scoop out nest called a redd. Center, salmon pair in spawning position. Quivering of male indicates shedding of milt. Of female's 2000 to 4000 eggs only a few will become mature fish. Bottom, salmon dying after spawning. Turbid water begins to clear about a day after a storm and fish then can be observed for the spawning period of two or three days.

female salmon is mostly a speckled dull green hue, as are steelhead of both sexes.

During the instinctive ritual the female seeks a gravel bed and with her body scoops out a shallow pit to receive her eggs. Males push upstream or drift down tail-first until they find likely mates. Each female salmon may attract a retinue of two or three large males and the same number of much smaller precocious males known as grilse.

This group maintains position just downstream from her. Battles ensue: the large males vie to shed their milt to fertilize the eggs as they are laid, the grilse harass them, the big ones dart at the grilse to drive them off.

Then, dying of vascular and other changes induced by spawning, the salmon retreat to deep pools and eventually are carried downstream, perhaps to lodge on the bank and provide the raccoons with a feast. Steelhead undergo similar degeneration which is mysteriously reversed, permitting most of them to return to the sea. Some live to spawn three times.

The new generation will hatch in about two months, remain in the gravel two weeks more, and then emerge to begin its fight for survival.

At noon on winter solstice the sun remains low. There is a hush in the forest, silver light on the stream, a flash of orange from the visiting varied thrush. Fronds of licorice fern decorate many bigleaf maples (above).

Botanically an epiphyte, this fern grows attached to moss on the tree but does not draw nourishment from it, instead producing its own food. The fresh roots smell like licorice, hence the name. In late spring both moss and fern wither; with the coming of autumn rains they thrive again.

Winter Light

Coral fungus

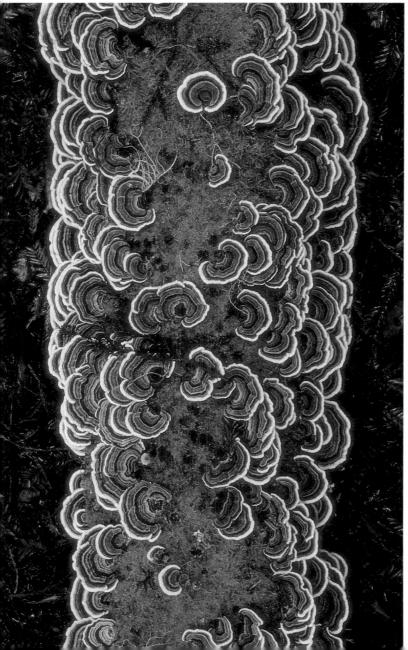

Time of the Fungi

As rains soak the forest floor, intriguing fungi begin to appear. There are at least 100 kinds of mushrooms in Muir Woods. Some pop up overnight; others take days to grow. Some last only a few hours; others remain for weeks. Most are cream or tan but a few are gaudy. Several are edible (although not to be picked); the rest are dubious or even deadly fare.

These plants play a clean-up role in the forest. Hidden beneath the growing surface is the main part of the plant called the mycelium, a mass of filaments that feed on dead organic matter and thus help decay it. When the mycelium is sufficiently mature to reproduce, ample moisture induces it to push a fruiting body into the air. This is the growth we see. It releases countless spores, a few of which will alight in receptive places and begin the cycle anew.

Different in behavior and rarely seen is slime mold, a mass of protoplasm on the surface of decaying vegetation.

Turkey-tail

Mycena on redwood cone

60

Red hygrophorus mushrooms

Gem-studded puffballs

Slime mold

Oyster mushrooms

Witch's butter

61

Upper Forest

Lost in their own silent world of cloud, these large redwoods stand astride a lofty part of the ridge on the west side of Redwood Canyon. Here the trees have little shelter and intercept summer fog and the full force of winter gales. Now a late winter storm has cloaked the mountain in mist. After the disturbance has passed, the view from the forest edge to the ocean emerges in wind-swept clarity. Hills that were brown in autumn now are green again.

Only a few hikers visit this hidden outpost nearly 1100 feet (335 meters) above the sea. The Dipsea and Ben Johnson trails climb to the fire road that runs through the forest.

Winter lingers at a hidden outpost high above the sea.

Signs of Spring

First flower to bloom is fetid adders-tongue (top left), named for its shape and rank odor. It appears early in January and blends with the forest floor. At top is California toothwort, commonly called rainbells, showing in February.

Above is western wake-robin, a trillium (for its three leaves) whose blooming in March heralds the true beginning of spring. The two flowers are in different stages: the blossom is white at first and gradually turns lavender. At left is the scarcer giant wake-robin, also a trillium, actual size.

On the opposite page, budding hazel and azalea leaves form a delicate screen behind the upturned base of a fallen redwood.

Now daylight hours increase rapidly and there is an explosion of life in the woods. A pregnant doe browses on the canyon floor and a satyr anglewing butterfly rests on slim solomon plume. A fern fiddlehead unrolls, miner's lettuce is lush in the lower canyon, and cow parsnip presents its white flower sprays. Redwood violet adds flecks of yellow to the forest floor.

New leaves of alders and bigleaf maples (opposite page) are ablaze with the golden hue of substances crucial to life, the carotenoids. Gradually the green coloring will darken as two kinds of chlorophyll increase. Sunlight acting on these green pigments will enable the leaves to use water from the soil and carbon dioxide from the air to manufacture food and oxygen, the process of photosynthesis that sustains all living things.

But paradoxically the light apparently would destroy the chlorophylls and related life-giving cells except for the protection provided by the carotenoids.

In fall, especially on the maples, yellows will reappear as green fades from the dying leaves.

The Days Lengthen...

...and Complete the Circle

In May clintonia's pink blooms dot the woods. A steady knocking and strident *wek-wek-wek* announce the presence of a pileated woodpecker, a resident often seen at this time of year and a bird much admired by Muir. Here one attacks the bark of a dead alder in search of insects. Fawns and their mothers appear; the doe is browsing elk clover already grown tall. Fog drifts in again. And (opposite) the year's new redwood needles add their bright note as summer returns to the forest.

THE LOWER CANYON

TREE LIFE changes as Redwood Canyon widens at its lower end. Redwoods at the Monument entrance (opposite, pollen-tinted) overlook smaller trees occupying the flat ground. Three species besides bay laurel are prominent in this bordering wood.

One is California buckeye, a member of the horse-chestnut family. The path between the two parking areas threads a whimsical world of its twisted branches best seen in winter when leaves have dropped. It flowers profusely in May and June and the hard fruit (above) drops from its pod in late fall. Local Coast Miwoks called the tree *ah*-tay and in lean years pulverized the fruit, leached out a toxic substance and cooked the resulting mush for food.

Coast live oaks display their sturdy limbs (top right). At left, red alders line the creek bottom; the sapwood turns red when exposed to air, thus the name. Alders reproduce by seed spread from fruiting cones, shown actual size. This deciduous tree is a familiar companion of coastal streams.

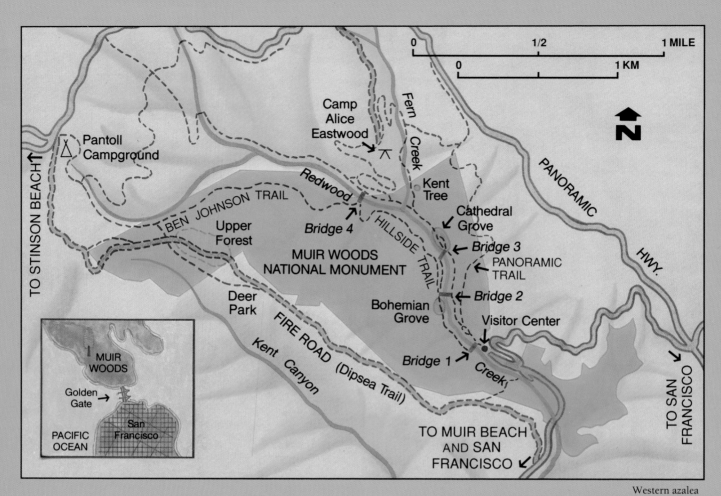

Western azalea

ABOUT THE AUTHOR

James Morley is a Bay Area native who has enjoyed observing and photographing Muir Woods for over 20 years. This is an all-color revision of his highly-acclaimed black and white book on the woods. His photographs have appeared on a best-selling poster and on a National Passport stamp of the Park Service. He also has evoked memories of the California gold rush in his book *Gold Cities*. He seeks to combine his pictures with facts in a way that touches on the wonder of it all.

ACKNOWLEDGMENTS

The courteous cooperation of the site manager and staff of Muir Woods National Monument, particularly of ranger Mia Monroe, was invaluable. National Park Service researcher Stephen D. Veirs, Jr. was extremely helpful, as were the following: David Arora; Bill Bigg, Humboldt State University; Lawson Brainerd; the California Academy of Sciences; Catherine A. Callaghan, Ohio State University; Faith L. Duncan; Fabrizio Camera Graphics; Felix Finch; Florida Museum of Natural History; the Griffins; Wes Hildreth; Bill and Phyllis Hogan; the Michael Hughes family; Bob Jones; J.P. Color Lab; Bill Libby and Joe R. McBride, University of California; Marin County Library; Joe Marshall; Ron Mastrogiuseppe, Redwood National Park; Charles Miller, University of Montana; Randy Millikin; Goro Mitchell; Thomas Morley, University of Minnesota; James Musser; Bob Petrule; Proteus Typography; Don Reeser; Salem Rice; Kim Rodriguez; Save-the-Redwoods League; the Shaffs; Shannon Sinnock; John Stuart, Humboldt State University; Larry Weeks; Jack A. Wolfe, U.S. Geological Survey; the Ray Wong family. Norm Slama and Liz Wegenka measured heights of several trees. Many others contributed. A hearty thanks to all! The author assumes responsibility for errors.

Historic photographs courtesy of the following: Pages 4 and 38, Society of California Pioneers; pages 6, 7, 9 (Muir) and 32, National Park Service; page 9 (Kent), Bancroft Library; page 11, Palo Alto Public Library; page 29, Dr. Andrew G. Jameson, Librarian–Historiographer, Bohemian Club; page 35, James A. Lawrence, photographer of that event.

Color photograph at top left of page 21 by Stephen D. Veirs, Jr., courtesy National Park Service. Ticket on page 38 courtesy National Park Service. Drawings are by Richard Waldron.

Quotations: Page 6, Muir letter, from William Kent Family Papers, Manuscripts and Archives, Yale University Library; page 26, from *The Outermost House* by Henry Beston, copyright 1956 by Henry Beston, Henry Holt and Company, Inc.; page 43, from *My First Summer in the Sierra Nevada* by John Muir, Houghton Mifflin Company.

Especially useful references were *Flowers and Ferns of Muir Woods* by Gladys L. Smith; *The Silva of California* by Willis L. Jepson; *William Kent, Independent* by Elizabeth T. Kent.

AUTHOR'S NOTE

The felling of most of the ancient redwood forests tells of our old illusion that natural resources are endless, that there is no need for limits, no need to think of tomorrow. George Perkins Marsh addressed the consequences of this attitude in his 1864 landmark book *Man and Nature*, which for the first time raised the issue of prudent use of resources. His work, at least as much as Muir's, helped persuade Theodore Roosevelt's administration (1901-1909) to enact many conservation measures, and probably helped set the climate for T. R.'s acceptance of Muir Woods.